THE BLAME GAME IN RELATIONSHIPS:

how to stop the blame game in your relationship

Robert A. Taylor

table of contents

Chapter 1: What Is the Blame Game?

Picture a classroom where scholars are working on a group design. The deadline is approaching, but they're far from finished and the schoolteacher is enquiring about the status of the design.

As the scholars start to explain themselves, " the blame game " begins. Everyone starts to point fritters at each other and the discussion goes around in circles as they try to avoid the blame and just put it on someone else.

Does this situation feel familiar? Have you endured something analogous, at work maybe? You've presumably indeed watched the blame game unfold on the news when there's a disaster, and politicians and directors fall each over themselves trying to shift the blame onto everyone but themselves.

" When people face impacts or unintended consequences after making a mistake, their fear may cause them to defend themselves by shifting the blame down from themselves and onto a goat, ".

This book explores reasons why people play the blame game, and how it can impact the people involved.

● Reasons People Play the blame Game

Here are some reasons why people play the blame game.

• Avoid Responsibility

People find themselves in this dynamic if they try to detach or part themselves from guilt when something goes wrong and their position has hovered. They try to avoid responsibility by shifting the blame onto someone else.

• cover Their Character

People tend to play the blame game when they sweat that retaining their miscalculations or taking responsibility for an error could negatively impact the way they're perceived.

These people tend to be insecure about their individualities and sweat that small mistakes could become global reflections of who they are, or that they could face disastrous consequences, like being fired.

- Signs of the blame Game

Occasionally it can be relatively apparent that someone is trying to shirk responsibility. Other times, it can be more subtle.

Here are some suggestions that someone is playing the blame game:

• Cutlet-pointing: People may point fritters at others. For example, they may say " Jill was supposed to shoot me the data for the graphs. I couldn't make the graphs without that information. "

• Denial: People may deny their responsibility. For example, they may say " No one told me we demanded to include graphs in the donation, how was I supposed to know? "

• Exclusion: People may constantly count on or marginalize a member of the group, and also make them the goat when things go wrong.

- Impact of the blame Game

Playing the blame game is unproductive and can lead to negative consequences.

• Impact on Situations

Shifting blame onto other people has a two-fold negative effect as it creates pressure and resentment in connections and diverts precious attention and coffers down from addressing the original problem.

People become protective and enkindle a vicious cycle of passing the buck and attacking each other, rather than banding together as a platoon to fix the problem through a result-acquainted approach.

• Impact on People

The blame game shapes how you view the world as you'll constantly be concerned with avoiding the burden of being responsible for wrongdoing, which takes precious energy down from forming strong connections with those around you.

Others are perceived as challengers rather than mates, which causes these folks to be insulated, less well-liked, and misdoubted. In turn, these people produce tone-fulfilling prognostics, as others will view them as selfish, and be less inclined to help them or endorse on their behalf in the wake of unborn miscalculations, further centralizing them against others.

There's an aspect of righteous outrage when it comes to blaming and how it makes others feel staid in comparison to the person at fault. Blame is a negative experience that can be painful and humiliating for the person who's assigned fault. Not only does it hurt the person, but it does little good beyond social comparison and diverts vital coffers down from the original issue.

• Impact on Organizations

Over time, a culture of blame and negativity at an association can cause the association to suffer. It can inhibit creativity and invention, as people are too spooked to try things for fear of impacts if something goes wrong.

It can also cause other stakeholders similar as guests and suppliers to lose faith in the association. For example, if a client calls because they have an issue and the response is " That error was made by someone in the account, we're the operations platoon and we can't do anything about it, " there's bound to be frustration.

A lot of problems may also go unaddressed, because people may be too hysterical to report them and face the blame. This can lead to a lot of inefficiency in associations, as people may find it easier to pretend there aren't any problems rather.

Chapter 2: Why Every wedded Couple Should Avoid The Blame Game

Playing the blame game is an unhealthy and dangerous way for couples to approach problem-working. Rather than resolving conflicts, blame and cutlet-pointing actually make them worse. However, in an intimate marriage, you'll want to avoid blaming each other for problems in your life, If you're trying to make or maintain a healthy relationship.

Let's look at some reasons why blame is so poisonous to our marriages.
1. blame Doesn't listen.

When you blame one another for a problem you're facing – big or small – you are laboriously choosing not to listen to your partner's side of the story. This hurts your capability to be humane and to hear them out when they explain their side.
However, also you can't get past the problem at hand If you can't walk in your partner's shoes to find out where they're coming from or what you may have misunderstood.

Harkening is one of the most important chops couples need to develop – as beforehand as possible. Because when you refuse to hear – blaming your partner for something that might not be their fault – you damage what might else be a healthy relationship.

2. Blame Assumes The Worst.

Blaming your partner for something they might not be responsible for means that, at least at the moment, you're assuming the worst of them. Think about it this way: if your partner always acted in your worst interests, would you have married them? presumably not.

Assuming the worst of your partner isn't a loving station to have. When you find yourself tempted to make snap hypotheticals, pause to consider what light you're painting them in. Taking the time to put your hypotheticals on hold will help you approach the situation with lesser clarity.

3. Blame Puts Your Partner in a Protective Position.

You and your partner will have a hard time working problems out if one of you is always on the guard. When you cast blame on one another, guard is a natural result. That's because blaming is always an obnoxious move.

When you force your partner to take a protective position, you effectively place a fresh hedge between yourselves and the problem you're trying to break. Blame and guard are extraneous obstacles you also have to overcome before you can get to the heart of the matter. However, avoid cutlet- pointing – and don't go on the descent, If you want to break the problem briskly.

4. Blame Damages Emotional Safety.

Emotional safety is a critically important element in healthy marriages. However, automatically assume the worst of them, and keep them in a protective position, If you don't listen to your partner in tough situations.

When you damage the emotional safety in your relationship, that negatively affects trust and intimacy. However, establish habits that nurture emotional safety and exclude habits – like blame – that hurt it, If you value your partner's trust and the closeness you enjoy.

Blame isn't a loving thing to do to anyone, and it has no place in marriage. It can occasionally be used as a control tactic. In some cases, blaming is an outside protuberance of our own internalized fears or precariousness.

Chapter 3: How blaming Can Destroy Intimacy

One of the most potent adversaries of quality connections is the use of blaming to win an argument. Yet, despite its predictable, toxic goods, couples regularly blame one another during their controversies.

- Free- For- All blaming Patterns

In these dangerous exchanges, both mates charge one another with a righteous passion to abate the other's point of view. Who's " more right " and who's " more wrong " is mooted about until the argument ultimately loses its intensity, and some kind of grace period follows. These free-for-all battles most frequently end in some kind of complementary " draw. " Both mates walk down feeling righteous in their positions, but frequently also sad about hurting the other.

Because the mates in these conflict patterns frequently feel both right and wrong, they generally don't consider their controversies as cumulatively damaging, yet that frequently turns out to be a false supposition.

With multiple reiterations of the same kinds of relations, both mates lose confidence in any kind of true resolution and act out these patterns with little conscious mindfulness.

Over time, they come vulnerable to their assignments of blame responsibility and are unfit to come up with any kind of robotic or innovative results that will keep these repetitious conflicts from recreating.

• Staggered blaming Patterns

This type of conflict pattern is more complicated and also more cumulatively dangerous. In these kinds of relations, the same mate constantly plays the part of the blamer while the argument is passing, but once the disagreement is over, they're also criticized by the other mate for the part they played during the conflict.

Within these controversies, the blamer indeed appears to hold all the cards, intent and successful in dismembering and erasing the other mate's point of view. also when the air clears, the subdued, putatively accepting-of-blame mate gets indeed latterly by withholding closeness, demanding harmonious rehashing of the argument, attacking the other mate for demanding to win at any cost, or martyring themselves and holding the other mate responsible for the pain foisted.

Still, blaming of any kind is a dangerous sport that can cumulatively damage all involved, If not stopped. Nonetheless, numerous couples continue to share in it anyhow.

When I observe these relations in comforting sessions, I frequently ask questions like " Why do you think you continue to be locked into this destructive pattern of demanding to demonstrate who the' bad joe' is? `` " How do you think your conflicts would change if blame was never part of your conflicts again? "

Do you and your mate interact in blaming conflict patterns, whether they're a free-for-all or staggered process? Can you imagine barring blame from your arguments from now on?

To change these negative blaming patterns, you must both agree that you want to learn how to stop them in any unborn arguments. It doesn't matter which kind of blaming part you play. It's a zero-sum game.

The good news is that, in utmost connections, blaming is easy to identify and abolish. And utmost couples, once they understand its constantly negative goods, want to leave it before.

Still, these are the ways to take If you and your mate are ready to stop this mutually sabotaging pattern.

1. Explore where and how your blaming behavior patterns began.

2. Come apprehensive of the triggers that cause you to blame — or to fold in its presence.

3. Partake those triggers with your mate, so that they can search for different ways to avoid them.

4. Fete and admit responsibility when you actually do something that your mate feels is hurtful, indeed if you didn't mean to cause any detriment.

● How blaming behavior Begins

- The Partner Who Too Readily Accepts blame

Before you can stop automatically feeling like you're at fault, you must realize how you learned to accept that as your fate, and why you continue to do so in your current relationship.

Those who too readily accept blame are frequently touched off by a mate who treats them as though they don't have a right to alter the argument's direction.
They feel equivocal between how they " should " bear as a " good " person, and they feel protective when told their studies or passions are unhappy.
Because they've been emotionally carved as children to always bear appropriately, they're fluently intimidated by feeling like they aren't okay in the eyes of the other, indeed when they're in a grown-up- to grown-up commerce.

launch at the morning of your life when you first came apprehensive of blame, and recall how you were forced to accept being wrong in any grueling commerce. Did your caretakers incontinently abate your defenses? Did they withdraw their love when you didn't measure up to their prospects?

The trouble of emotional abandonment terrifies children. When faced with that possible consequence, they frequently become automatic acceptors of blame, carrying in whatever ways they can to be in the other's good graces again. They internalize the feeling that their caretakers were right to discipline them.

Still, you're likely, as a grown-up, you endured these kinds of relations when you were a child and believed that you merited them. Under attack, you may try to maintain your point of view, but feel defeated from the morning.

Staying for the conflict to end, you may reclaim your own worth by allowing yourself to feel the anger of being unfairly indicted and also look for ways to retaliate that unfairness and avenge.

- The Partner Who Is the Blamer

When blamed or challenged, blamers tend to incontinently reply in an accusatory way. maybe fearful of being criticized, they're urgently driven to make certain that they're never wrong. They may use their physical elevation to intimidate, their emotional power to dominate, or their intellectual delivery to invalidate.

The accepting- of- blame mate will frequently essay to stop the blaming by either fleetly capitulating, defending, decoupling, or promising to do better. Rather than stop the blaming, those postures most frequently actually increase it. Once the blaming pattern has started, there's very little the other mate can do until the process ends.

Go back to your origins as a child. Did you substantiate emotional or physical bullying of this kind when conflicts arose? Did you identify with the person who was groveling, but never wanted to be like that person? Did you covenant to emulate the more important person, or did you identify more with the one who gave in?

When you're challenged in a conflict, do you feel that you must incontinently dominate, or you'll lose? When your mate gives in to your need to end up on top, do you feel poorly latterly for doing what you've done? Are you angry at your mate for not standing up for themselves?

Numerous equate the most frequently " criticized " mate, who is flaunting tone-defeating or repressed hostility behavior, with womanish energy, and the tone-righteous mate as having further manly energy. Clearly, where there's a power difference that's blatant within a relationship, manly energy is more competitive and hierarchical, while womanish energy is more directed to collaboration and harmony-seeking.

In nonage surroundings, further adaptation, adaption, and harmonious behavior are anticipated from youthful girls than from youthful boys in utmost families.
Women who have been anticipated and/ or awarded to " give in " as children have to work very hard to change those actions as they develop. Men who were given the right to fight harder and with lower compassion than boys need to work just as hard to learn modesty and chivalry under attack.

In reality, I've seen both genders assuming this hourly-labeled wrong person part in the relationship. Men in our society aren't supposed to " give in " to a fight, so the marker may be more frequently assigned to that gender, but there are numerous women who fight- to palm and take no captures.
- Triggers

Whether you more frequently play the part of the blamer or the criticized, you're being touched off to respond by internalized recollections from your history. As stated over, whichever part you find yourself living out in your current relationship, ask yourself what your mate does that triggers you to respond the way you do. These actions can be emotional, physical, or intellectual.

This part of the mending process can be very problematic and must be entered into with the amenability of both mates to search for their own donation to this dysfunctional pattern. When a couple has been rehearsing blaming actions for a long time, it's typical for each of them to defend their actions by blaming the other for causing them to bear that way.

Occasionally, the mates who too readily accept blame are fearful of sharing their triggers. They need to believe that their preliminarily blaming mates won't use them as security in future conflicts. The blaming mates are generally not as upset, and therefore more willing to tell their mates what causes them to come angry.

Once triggers are shared and accepted, the mates must work diligently to exclude those automatic responses of blame or guilt. Each relationship is unique, but intimate mates who truly want to change are eager to substitute non-triggering actions when they know they cause detriment.

- Humility and Responsibility

Blame, in and of itself, is always a dangerous and hurtful behavior, no matter how it's expressed. There's only one way that both of the mates who are netted in blaming actions can stop them.
They must agree to replace them with reasonable and regardful requests at the moment and the amenability to accept what the other mate can offer, understanding completely that forced submission will never affect sustaining closeness.

All couples fight, And at times, it's ineluctable that they wound one another. But leaving blame before will significantly reduce those hurtful experiences.

You can begin the process of leaving blaming behavior behind if you and your mate can recognize the following five agreements

1. Still, invalidates the other's integrity, and defies agreements, If either mate does something that they know breaks trust.

2. Both mates will express genuine responsibility and remorse if they hurt the other.

3. Rather than rehashing arguments, they will barrage them by examining how they could have been more regardful and less threatening to the other during their previous conflict.

4. When either mate is touched off, they will ask the other to stop the current disagreement until that detector is reused. They agree that an emotional waterfall will sabotage any resolution and must be resolved before the conflict can happen.

5. They continuously remind each other that they can not resolve any disagreement when they're on opposing brigades.

Most of the couples who have espoused these agreements have been very successful in barring their blaming behaviors. However, you'll be truly astonished at how fleetly your dissensions will transfigure If you and your mate are willing to borrow them. As a conflict-successful couple, you'll be less likely to harm and further quick to heal.

Chapter 4: Why We blame Others

Do you find yourself blaming others when events don't unfold how you want them to? Once you blame someone, do you also think they earn to be treated or thought of inadequately? Do you notice this pattern repeating frequently in your life? If so, it's presumably because you're engaged in the blame game. This chapter will primarily concentrate on the cerebral reasons for blaming others, the reasons we do it, as well as ways to overcome this deformation.

Blame is defined as assigning responsibility for a fault or wrong. We blame others for a number of events and that made us late, she made me feel shamefaced, they dragooned me to make a decision, and he made me explode with rage. Blaming others leads to several harmful feelings, similar to resentment, anger, and abomination. We blame others for our actions, our studies, and our passions which are negative. I've yet to meet anyone who blames people for the good things that are in our lives.

● Why Do We Blame Others?

So why do people blame others?

The reason why people generally blame others is that it's a quick escape from guilt. Blame is an incredibly easy and royal tactic to use when we feel defensive.
Blame is frequently used by those of us who have a desire or need to be perfect. When agitating blame with guests, I find that guests who blame more generally have the illogical demand " I must/ought/ ought to be perfect and if I'm not, also I'm unworthy/ unloveable/ a failure/etc. " Holding ourselves responsible for our conduct generally puts us in a vulnerable position, and as a result, it can be delicate to do.
When we blame others, we refuse responsibility for our benefactions to the problem. Blaming other people is an easy eschewal and an easy way for us to continue our

actions, which may be the source of the problem we're hoping to put on someone else.

This denial of responsibility also denies us control of a given situation. Once I blame the MTA hand, the barista who makes my coffee at a crawler's pace, my mate, my parenting, my family, or my therapist, I can no longer change my circumstances because I'm thinking, " Well, I didn't do anything to cause my problem This was all her fault.

Blaming others keeps us from seeing ways we can alter our behavior to achieve an outgrowth, it leaves us helpless, and it stunts our particular growth.

This is obviously a state that we don't want to stay in permanently. By making others the responsible party for our problems, particular progress can be stalled.

In fact, when we choose to ignore any sign, big or small, regarding the relegation of blame, we can indeed find ourselves pushing down those who are coming from a place of support. Still, if we address the situation with the attention it deserves, it's much easier to read our own feelings and see the reason behind the beginning issue.

•How To Avoid The Habit Of Blaming

1. Stop buttressing your harmful thinking patterns. After a script arises in which you find yourself blaming someone, you'll probably want to pick up the phone and tell a friend about how stupidly this person conducted, complain to your associates about this person, or articulate to anyone who wants to hear.

Still, when we blame others and constantly relate the story to others, we support the blame and feelings from it. The coming time you blame someone, try to not relate the story at all to anyone and see how it affects you emotionally, mentally, or physically.

2. Change how you view miscalculations. Rather than viewing crimes as failures to be criticized by others, try to see them as openings for self-enhancement. By admitting your responsibility, you're more suitable to learn from your miscalculations and gain lesser control of your life.

3. See a therapist. As stated before in this blog, people who blame frequently have a fragile sense of tone- worth. They believe they can't make a mistake, as doing so would mean they're defective. Seeing a therapist will help you work towards accepting your mortal fallibility and capacity for error without demeaning yourself or avoiding holding yourself responsible.

Chapter 5: How to Stop the blame Game in Your Relationship

When you realize that you and your mate spend a lot of time playing the blame game in your relationship, it may be the right time to address this problem, see what's going on, and stop it altogether.

It can be a challenge to stop the blame game in nearly any relationship, but it's important to do so for both parties. Most people don't want to be criticized, whether they did something or not.

The blame game simply means that one person is blaming someone else for problems or issues that are passing, and they may be blaming the other person that they're in a relationship with.

For illustration, your mate may blame you for all the money problems you're passing, indeed if they spend as important money as you do. When you're talking about the blame game in connections, occasionally the person being criticized for the problem may actually be at fault, but in other cases, they may not be.

In other words, when a couple plays the blame game with each other, it may lead to problems because occasionally a person is actually diverting blame rather than being honest. This can lead to arguments or worse, so you should stop the blame game whenever this is possible.

● ways to stop the blame game in your relationship

Before understanding the ways to stop the blame game, it's essential to know why this problem occurs. Why do mates begin to blame each other rather than try to resolve the issue?

Think about these ways to stop the blame game to see if they will work well for your relationship.

1. Put yourself in your mate's shoes

When you're blaming your mate for something, imagine how they feel about the situation. Do you want to be criticized for things, indeed when you do them?

There's a good chance that you don't. So, your mate likely feels the same way. Maybe there's another way that you can handle the situation besides blaming someone. You should also think about what's going on in your mate's life.

Perhaps they didn't take out the trash or they forgot to call you because they have a big design problem at work, or they have a sick family member. Consider cutting your mate some slack occasionally, especially when they're stressed out or having a hard time in other aspects of their life.

2. Talk about things

When you're trying to learn how to stop blaming others, you should do your best to talk about things with your mate. However, this may be more productive than blaming them, If you're suitable to talk to them about the things that are bothering you or that you dislike.

Still, they may feel like they're being attacked and decide they don't want to talk to you about certain motifs presently If someone is telling them to stop blaming me and they haven't stopped.

Immaculately, you should have conversations before this happens, so you'll have a better chance of working things out with your mate, no matter what you're blaming each other over.

A 2019 study indicates that people anticipate someone to shift the blame, so that may not be the beginning problem in your relationship. It's necessary to determine what is, still, so you can continue to work through any issues you're facing.

3. Listen to your mate

When you take the time to bandy things with your mate, make sure that you're harkening to what they've to say. It isn't fair if you anticipate your mate to listen to you and you aren't doing the same for them.

This is a great way to stop the blame game and may help you see their point of view also. However, remember that their passions are just as valid as yours If they're telling you how they feel. You can decide together how to change your behavior
towards each other, in order to fix the problem, not the blame.

4. Focus on the things you have control over

Another thing you can do when you're trying to stop blaming others for your problems is to concentrate on the things that you have control over. However, think about ways you can change this without changing your mate's behavior, If you feel like it's your mate's fault that some things are passing.

To negotiate this, you may have to alter the way you are thinking about circumstances. rather than thinking something like, my partner is spending all of our money, try to figure out how to start budgeting, so you can make sure you aren't contributing to bad fiscal practices.

5. Talk about your places with each other

Commodity else you may want to bandy with your mate is what your prospects of each other are. However, you should do your best to determine what you want from each other, If your places weren't dilated out well on the morning of the relationship.

There's a chance that your mate doesn't know that you anticipate them to stay at home with you on the weekends, or you may not know that your mate likes the way you make sandwiches, so they ask you to make all their sandwiches.

When you're apprehensive of the logic behind the things that may lead to the blame game, it can be easier to work through them.

6. Let some things go

After you talk about what you anticipate from each other, it may be time to let some of the passions go that you have been passing.

Still, consider letting some of these hard passions go, If you consider your mate responsible for certain things that have happened in your relationship and you find out that they actually had a good reason for acting a specific way.

This may be a large step to help stop the blame game. Also, you should understand that some battles aren't worth fighting. However, don't blame them for this, If your mate forgets to flush the restroom occasionally. Just remember that they do this, so you can be prepared each time you enter the restroom.

There are some things that your mate does that may never change, and you should think about if these things are serious when you consider your entire relationship.

7. Don't take it personally

Occasionally you might think that your mate is doing things on purpose to upset you and make you blame them. There's a good chance that numerous of the things they're doing that might get on your jitters are moreover done by accident or absentmindedly.

You can't anticipate your mate to know what you want from them unless you express it to them. However, you shouldn't take their conduct personally unless they're done just to malign you If you haven't done that. However, you may have larger problems in your relationship, If you find that they are.

8. Get help

Once you determine you're unfit to stop the blame game, you might want to consider taking advantage of professional help to get to the bottom of things.

In remedy, you and your mate will be suitable to bandy why they might think not to put the blame on me, and why you feel that blaming them is justified, or the other way around.

Still, you may still be suitable to see benefits on your own, If your mate is unintentionally going to a counselor with you. A therapist can help you learn how to act else in some situations, and educate you on tips on how to hear or communicate more effectively.

9. think about your conduct

You should always think about your conduct as well. Are there things that you should be criticized for that your mate lets slide?

Maybe you blame your mate indeed if some things are your fault. However, think about why this is the case If either of these things is true. You may be hysterical about getting criticized for things, indeed if they're your fault.

Being hysterical to take the blame may be something you need to work out and is another way a therapist can be of backing too. Take the time you need to think about your behavior to determine if it needs to be addressed and changed or not.

10. Keep going(or don't)

When you find it becoming too insolvable to stop the blame game in your relationship, you should think about if this relationship is working or not. However, do everything you can to work through your issues, If you want it to work.

You can start by reading further on the content of blaming people and how to stop, and also get professional advice when this is necessary.

On the other hand, if you don't think the relationship should move forward, you may want to think about other feasible options. Be honest with yourself and your mate about your decision and keep an open mind.

Consider other ways of handling the situation and if they indeed need to be worked out in the first place. Are the things that are bothering you a big deal?

Think about all the options you have, if you're doing anything you should be criticized for, or if your relationship could profit from comfort. All of these things may be suitable to change how and if you continue to blame each other, which can be a good thing.

Conclusion

When something goes wrong, it can be tempting to cover yourself and blame someone else. Still, the situation suffers if everyone is more concerned with assigning blame than finding a result. Playing the blame game can also lead to poisonous connections as people turn against each other and attack one another.

Rather, promoting particular responsibility, openness, a clear division of liabilities, and a result-concentrated approach is more productive.